WASHOE COUNTY LIBRARY

3 1235 03812 7689

P9-DUT-903

DRONES
EYES IN THE SKIES

CIVILIAN DRONES

DANIEL R. FAUST

PowerKiDS
press

New York

Published in 2016 by The Rosen Publishing Group, Inc.
29 East 21st Street, New York, NY 10010

Copyright © 2016 by The Rosen Publishing Group, Inc.

All rights reserved. No part of this book may be reproduced in any form without permission in writing from the publisher, except by a reviewer.

First Edition

Editor: Sarah Machajewski
Book Design: Reann Nye

Photo Credits: Cover dreamnikon/Shutterstock.com; p. 5 (White House) Andrea Izzotti/Shutterstock.com; p. 5 (drone) Maria Dryfhout/Shutterstock.com; p. 7 Oleg Yarko/Shutterstock.com; p. 8 AlexLMX/ Shutterstock.com; p. 9 R.Babakin/Shutterstock.com; p. 11 (helicopter) stockphoto mania/Shutterstock.com; p. 11 (airplane) Patryk Kosmider/Shutterstock.com; pp. 11, 17, 21 (background) mexrix/Shutterstock.com; p. 13 (hexacopter, quadcopter, RC transmitter) marekuliasz/Shutterstock.com; p. 13 (background) Reinhold Leitner/Shutterstock.com; p. 15 ERIC CABANIS/AFP/Getty Images; p. 17 (drone) Allen.G/ Shutterstock.com; p. 18 Thatsaphon Saengnarongrat/Shutterstock.com; p. 19 digidreamgrafix/ Shutterstock.com; p. 20 Thomas Pajot/Shutterstock.com; p. 23 (inset) Mike Hurd/Moment/Getty Images; p. 23 (main) N.Minton/Shutterstock.com; p. 25 alik/Shutterstock.com; p. 27 (background) kampee patisena/Moment Open/Getty Images; p. 27 (drone) https://commons.wikimedia.org/wiki/ File:Drone_surveillance_helps_search_and_rescue_in_Nepal_(17313224411).jpg; p. 28 Oleksiy Mark/ Shutterstock.com; p. 29 By Melissa M'Lou/Moment Open/Getty Images; p. 30 Skip Brown/ National Geographic/Getty Images.

Cataloging-in-Publication Data

Faust, Daniel R.
Civilian drones / by Daniel R. Faust.
p. cm. — (Drones: eyes in the skies)
Includes index.
ISBN 978-1-5081-4486-1 (pbk.)
ISBN 978-1-5081-4487-8 (6-pack)
ISBN 978-1-5081-4488-5 (library binding)
1. Drone aircraft — Juvenile literature. I. Faust, Daniel R. II. Title.
UG1242.D7 F38 2016
623.74'69—d23

Manufactured in the United States of America

CPSIA Compliance Information: Batch #BW16PK: For Further Information contact Rosen Publishing, New York, New York at 1-800-237-9932

CONTENTS

WHAT IS A DRONE?

You've probably seen or heard about drones in the news, but do you know what a drone is? "Drone" is another name for an unmanned aerial **vehicle**, or UAV. A UAV is an aircraft that operates without a human pilot aboard. UAVs are controlled by an onboard computer or through a remote control by a pilot on the ground or in another vehicle.

Historically, drones were used by the military for missions that were too dull, dirty, or **dangerous** for manned aircraft. However, in recent years, civilian drones have been developed to help firefighters, inspect buildings, deliver medicine, and more. Drone flying has even become a popular hobby, through machines such as remote-controlled airplanes. Many companies now sell drones that can be controlled with a smartphone.

CIVILIAN DRONES

"Civilian" means "not having to do with the military." Civilian drones are used by nonmilitary people. Drones have become a popular hobby.

In January 2015, a civilian drone landed on the White House lawn. Although it turned out to be harmless, police and the Secret Service were concerned for the safety of the First Family.

USES FOR DRONES

The first drones to make news were those used by the United States military. These drones, like the Predator, were used primarily for **surveillance** and **intelligence** gathering. Soon, military drones were equipped with missiles and other weapons and were being used for more offensive missions.

Although drones became famous through military uses, there are many ways civilians can use them. Civilian drones, sometimes called unmanned aerial systems (UASs), are used to survey land, inspect construction sites, take aerial photographs, or deliver supplies to otherwise hard-to-reach areas. Civilian drones are now even being used for recreational purposes, such as racing and aerial photography. Many companies sell drones for beginners that are ready to use right out of the box. You can even buy or make parts to **customize** your own drone.

DIFFERENT DRONE NAMES

The Federal Aviation Administration (FAA) uses the term "unmanned aircraft systems" to describe civilian drones.

Military drones, like the MQ-1 Predator, are equipped with surveillance equipment, such as video and photographic cameras. Infrared and radar allow the drone operator to see at night and through bad weather.

HOW DO DRONES FLY?

Drones come in many different shapes and sizes. Many civilian drones are based on the quadcopter design. A quadcopter is like a helicopter that is lifted and propelled by four helicopter rotors. Whatever their design, all drones rely on the same basic principles to get off the ground and stay in the air.

Like other aircraft, drones are able to fly because of four basic principles: lift, thrust, weight, and drag. Lift is the force that moves an aircraft upward. Thrust is the forward motion of an aircraft. Weight is the force created by the pull of gravity. Drag is the force produced by the **resistance** of the air against the aircraft's forward motion. The way these forces work together is what allows aircraft to fly.

MAKING IT LIGHT

Civilian drones are usually made of lightweight materials, such as plastic. Light materials mean less power is needed to keep the drone in the air.

ROTOR

A rotor is the part of a helicopter that turns, which helps lift a helicopter off the ground.

Drones can be either fixed wing, like airplanes, or rotary wing, like helicopters. Fixed-wing aircraft have wings that stay in place. Rotary-wing aircraft have wings, or rotors, that move.

Fixed-wing drones need thrust to be greater than drag in order to move forward. When this happens, air moves under the wings, creating lift. When the force of lift becomes greater than the aircraft's weight, the aircraft moves upward.

Helicopters and other rotorcraft don't need forward thrust to create lift. The blades on a helicopter's rotor are shaped like narrow wings, and their rapid rotation makes the lift needed to get the aircraft off the ground. Tilting the rotors allows the rotorcraft to move forward, backward, or side to side.

This diagram shows the different ways that thrust, lift, weight, and drag act upon fixed-wing and rotary-wing aircraft. Like other aircraft, drones rely on these same forces.

FIXED–WING AIRCRAFT

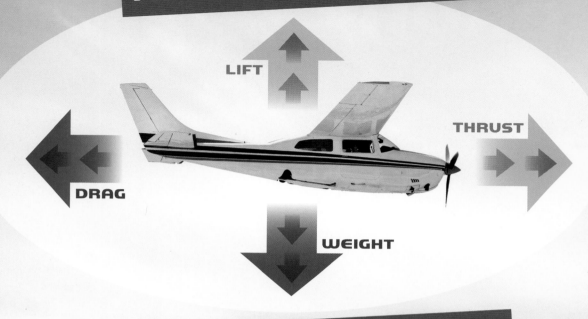

LIFT

THRUST

DRAG

WEIGHT

ROTARY–WING AIRCRAFT

THRUST
LIFT

WEIGHT
DRAG

DRONE PARTS

Whether your civilian drone is a fixed-wing UAV or a rotorcraft, most have the same basic **components**. The most common frames are quadcopters, meaning they have space for four rotors. If a drone needs to carry a camera or other heavy load, it needs to have more rotors.

The "brain" of the drone is the flight controller, or autopilot. Flight controllers help **stabilize** the drone. Some flight controllers can be programmed to fly the drone along a preset flight path. If something goes wrong with the flight controller, an RC transmitter and receiver act as good backup. These parts are controlled **manually**.

The flight controller and rotors need a power source. Lithium polymer batteries are the most common because they're lightweight, but provide a lot of power. Most civilian drones use three or four batteries.

HEXACOPTER

QUADCOPTER

RC TRANSMITTER

RC RECEIVER

Hexacopters, such as the top drone, have six rotors. Octocopters have eight. The heavier the drone, the more rotors it needs to produce enough lift to get off the ground.

CONTROLLING DRONES

There are two ways to control a civilian drone: by remote control or through an onboard flight controller. A remote-controlled drone operates the same way a remote-controlled airplane does. An operator uses a handheld radio transmitter that communicates with a receiver inside the drone. The receiver controls the equipment on the aircraft based on what the operator tells it to do.

Even if a drone is controlled by remote control, it still has the equipment needed to operate under **autonomous** flight. In addition to the flight controller, many drones also include a GPS, sensors, stabilizers, and computer software that programs the drone's flight path. There are several different programs you can use to program a drone's flight from your computer, tablet, or mobile phone.

THERE'S AN APP FOR THAT!

Some drones come with software that allows you to control them through Wi-Fi with a smartphone or tablet, but you'll need to download the app to begin. If the drone has a camera, you can stream or record video directly to your mobile device.

The woman in this photograph is using a handheld transmitter to control the drone. Even if you have a preprogrammed flight controller, it's a good idea to have a handheld controller as backup.

TRICKED-OUT DRONES

One of the best things about owning a drone is customizing it however you want. Some of these additions help the drone perform specific tasks, while others just make it look cool.

If you want to use your drone to take pictures or record videos, you'll need to add a camera. Many out-of-the-box quadcopters are powerful enough to carry most small consumer cameras. You can further customize your camera drone by adding a stabilizing gimbal, which is a part that helps steady the camera while the drone is in flight.

Some of the most tricked-out drones are those used for first-person-view (FPV) drone racing. Racers fly drones that have been customized with LED lights and performance accessories to see which one is the fastest. Some multirotor drones can go more than 37 miles (59.5 km) per hour!

READY TO RACE!

First-person-view (FPV) drone racing is an exciting way to use your drone. Racers wear goggles that show them what the drone sees as it's flying through the air.

GIMBAL

This drone's camera is attached to a gimbal. The gimbal holds the camera steady while the drone is in the air, reducing the effects of vibrations and shaking.

SAFETY FIRST!

Drone flying can be a lot of fun. Like most activities, it's important to follow simple safety rules to avoid hurting yourself or others. There are many safety guidelines that recreational drone operators must follow.

First, make sure you're familiar with the way your drone works and how to operate it correctly before using it in public. Check if there are any safety guidelines dealing with flying remote-controlled aircraft in your area, such as specific times of day or places where remote-controlled aircraft, like your drone, are allowed to be flown. It's important to remember that laws keep people from flying drones higher than 400 feet (122 m) and that you must keep your drone in sight at all times.

Before taking your drone out for its first flight, call a local remote-controlled aircraft club. They'll be able to tell you about safety guidelines in your area.

It's your responsibility to make sure your drone isn't a danger to others. You must keep your drone at least 25 feet (7.6 m) away from other people. Never fly over moving vehicles on purpose. If you live within 5 miles (8 km) of an airport, it's your responsibility to contact the airport before flying your drone. Never use your drone to get in the way of manned aircraft.

You must remember to keep your drone away from private property. You should never photograph or spy on people without their permission. Never fly your drone near dangerous areas, such as construction sites and busy roadways. Stay away from secure facilities like power stations and government buildings.

DRONE DOS & DON'TS

DO

Fly in an open area.

Fly your drone for personal enjoyment.

Take lessons and learn to fly your drone safely.

Contact the airport when flying within 5 miles (8 km) of the airport.

DON'T

Fly near manned aircraft.

Allow your drone to fly beyond your line of sight.

Use your drone to spy on people.

Ignore local or community-based safety guidelines.

You might think it'd be fun to see if your drone can keep up with a larger aircraft. But it's dangerous and illegal to use a drone to interfere with manned aircraft, such as airplanes and helicopters.

DRONES AND AERIAL PHOTOGRAPHY

Cameras are something commonly added to drones. Many consumer cameras are light enough to be carried by small drones. There are many fun activities for you and your friends to enjoy with a drone-mounted camera. Of course, you must always remember to respect the privacy of those around you.

Have you and your friends ever wanted to make a movie? Imagine the fun aerial shots your movie could include if you filmed it with a drone-mounted camera instead of a regular handheld camera. Or maybe you're a fan of extreme sports such as skiing, snowboarding, or **BASE jumping**. A drone-mounted camera is the perfect way to get up close and personal with your friends during these activities.

Drones are a fun way to take exciting videos of you and your friends. But if you're thinking of selling your photographs or videos, you'll need a special license from the FAA.

FARMING AND ENVIRONMENTAL USES

Because drones can fly several hundred feet above the ground, they're the perfect way to survey large areas of land. Farmers can use drones to check their fields and identify the areas that require water, fertilizer, or **pesticides**. Drones can even be used as **crop dusters**. Ranchers can use drones to monitor their herds or search for missing animals.

Scientists can use drones to study weather patterns and ocean currents. Drones can be sent inside a hurricane, which is far too dangerous for a manned aircraft. Archaeologists can use drones to explore and diagram excavation sites from the air. Environmental groups use drones to monitor pollution levels and deforestation. Drones are also used by animal rights groups, like the World Wildlife Fund, to monitor, track, and protect endangered animals as well as to fight **poachers**.

DRONES VS. POACHERS

A group called Air Shepherd uses drones to fight elephant and rhino poachers in Africa. They use drones to identify and track these illegal hunters across Africa's vast landscape. The data collected by these drones is sent to nearby rangers, who then arrest the poachers.

Farmers own a lot of land. It can be expensive to properly monitor all that land, which is why some farmers have started to use drones to help them inspect their fields.

DRONES FOR CONSTRUCTION AND MORE

The uses for civilian drones are endless. For example, during the height of the Occupy Wall Street movement in 2011, a drone known as the "Occucopter" was used to stream live video of protests.

Construction companies use drones to improve communication, efficiency, and safety. Drones are being used to assess construction sites, inspect dangerous or hard-to-reach sections of a building, and provide added security at job sites.

Drones are also being used to save lives. S.W.A.R.M. (Search with Aerial RC Multirotor) is a worldwide group of volunteers who use drones to help locate missing persons. It takes a single drone minutes to search several square miles. It would take a human search party several hours to search the same area.

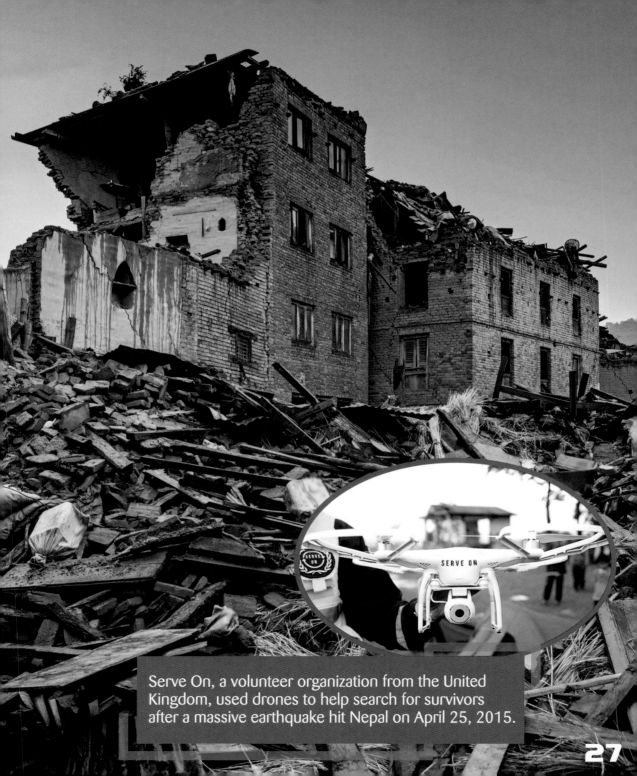

Serve On, a volunteer organization from the United Kingdom, used drones to help search for survivors after a massive earthquake hit Nepal on April 25, 2015.

BUILD OR BUY?

Now that you've seen all the fun things drones can do, you probably want to run out and start flying your own drone. But should you buy a drone or try to build your own?

The obvious advantage to buying a drone is that you can start having fun as soon as you take it out of the box. If you're just interested in flying a drone around and shooting some videos, then buying a drone might be the best option for you. Many manufacturers sell beginner models for under $100.

3D PRINTING YOUR DRONE

You've probably heard about 3D printers. Did you know 3D printers are a great way to build drones? If you have access to a 3D printer, you can use it to build your drone's frame, landing gear, and propellers. You'll still need to buy the batteries and motors, though.

Drones may look **complicated**, but don't let that keep you from building your own. You can buy the parts you need online or from a local hobby shop. You can even print your own parts with a 3D printer.

If you're interested in knowing how every part of your drone works, then building your own drone from scratch might be best. Getting the basic parts will cost you about the same as a premade drone, but you'll have the option of modifying and improving your drone as you build it.

TOYS OR TOOLS?

Just a few years ago, drones were something straight out of a science-fiction movie. Today, drones are very real, and they're only going to get more common each year as we find more and more uses for these small flying machines.

Whether you build your own drone from 3D-printed parts or buy a premade drone online, you can take to the air right now. While you can use your drone for fun, recreational activities or to help others, it's always important to follow the rules and keep yourself and those around you safe. And who knows? You might enjoy operating a drone so much that you decide to make it your future career.

GLOSSARY

autonomous: Not controlled by others or by outside forces.

BASE jumping: An extreme sport in which someone parachutes from a variety of fixed objects, specifically tall buildings, antennas, bridges, and natural formations.

complicated: Involving many different and confusing aspects.

component: A part of a mechanical or electrical system.

crop duster: A light aircraft used for spraying crops with pesticide.

customize: To build or change to suit a certain purpose.

dangerous: Likely to cause harm or injury.

intelligence: The collection of information that is of military or political value.

manually: Worked by hand, not automatically or electronically.

pesticide: A substance used for killing bugs or other creatures that are harmful to plants and animals.

poacher: A person who hunts illegally.

resistance: Any force that opposes motion.

stabilize: To make stable.

surveillance: Continuous observation of a person, place, or group in order to gather information.

vehicle: A machine that is powered to move on its own.

INDEX

WEBSITES

Due to the changing nature of Internet links, PowerKids Press has developed an online list of websites related to the subject of this book. This site is updated regularly. Please use this link to access the list: www.powerkidslinks.com/dron/civi